IMAGES
of America

CAPE HATTERAS
NATIONAL SEASHORE

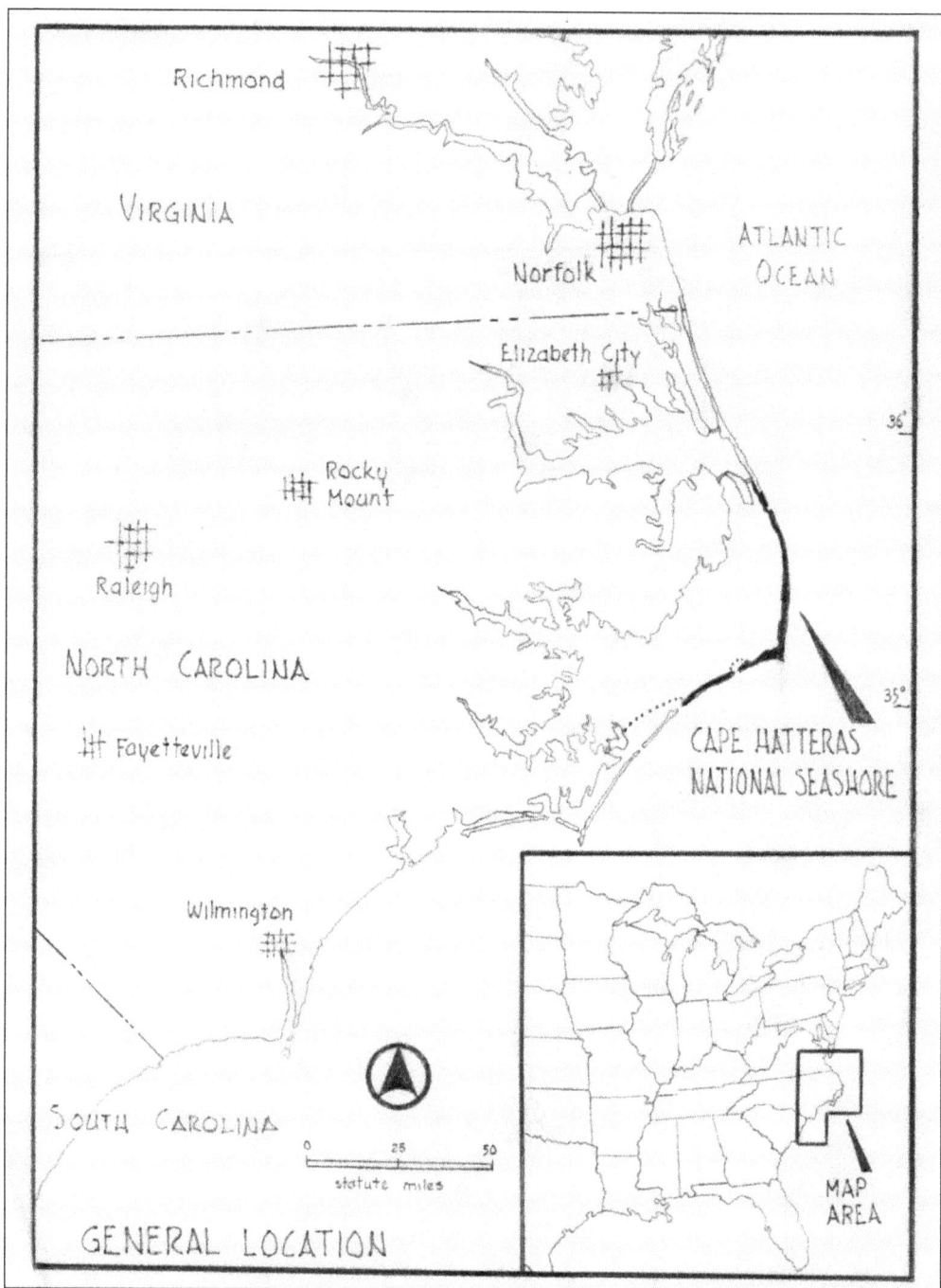

This early-1950s map of the North Carolina coast shows the location of the creation and establishment of Cape Hatteras National Seashore in North Carolina. This is the official map used in the planning document for the seashore. (Courtesy of the National Park Service.)

ON THE COVER: In this 1950s photograph, park visitors enjoy South Beach with the Cape Hatteras Lighthouse in the background. (Courtesy of the National Park Service/Cape Hatteras National Seashore.)

IMAGES
of America

CAPE HATTERAS
NATIONAL SEASHORE

Douglas Stover

ARCADIA
PUBLISHING

Published by Arcadia Publishing
Charleston, South Carolina

Library of Congress Control Number: 2014949517

For all general information, please contact Arcadia Publishing:
Telephone 843-853-2070
Fax 843-853-0044
E-mail sales@arcadiapublishing.com
For customer service and orders:
Toll-Free 1-888-313-2665

Visit us on the Internet at www.arcadiapublishing.com

CONTENTS

ACKNOWLEDGMENTS

I am pleased to present this collection of historic images of Cape Hatteras National Seashore, which was assembled with the help of many sources and research material from the Cape Hatteras National Seashore Museum Resource Center in Manteo, North Carolina. Special thanks to Jami Lanier, museum technician, Outer Banks Group, National Park Service, for sharing her knowledge of history and the museum collection at Cape Hatteras National Seashore and for allowing me to spend so much time in the collection looking over more than 500 historic photographs. I want to thank Jami for reviewing and editing the photographs and text. Many thanks to Cyndy Holda, public affairs specialist, Outer Banks Group, National Park Service (and local Outer Banker), for sharing her time and knowledge in reviewing this book.

Special thanks to Sarah Downing, assistant curator, and Stuart Parks, archivist, from The Outer Banks History Center, a North Carolina State regional archives and research library in Manteo. Thank you to Sarah for finding a photograph of Frank Stick and to Stuart for scanning the photograph. I want to thank Katie McAlpin-Owens, my acquisitions editor, and the production staff at Arcadia Publishing for allowing me to research and write this book and working with me through the stages of publication.

I would also like to credit Cameron Binkley, author of "The Creation and Establishment of Cape Hatteras National Seashore: The Great Depression through Mission 66." (Mission 66 was a federally sponsored program to improve deteriorated structures and visitor experiences in the national parks, the result of a massive visitor boom to the parks after World War II.) Thanks to his research, I was provided with background information that I used throughout this book.

Unless otherwise noted, all images appear courtesy of the National Park Service (NPS)/Cape Hatteras National Seashore.

INTRODUCTION

The Cape Hatteras National Seashore, administered by the National Park Service, consists of 70 miles of beach stretching from Nags Head to Ocracoke, North Carolina. Each year, more than two million people visit the seashore to enjoy its beaches, fish, swim, surf, bird-watch, or visit one of the seashore's lighthouses (Bodie Island, Cape Hatteras, and Ocracoke). The islands of Cape Hatteras National Seashore are constantly being changed by wind, tides, and storms; these islands contain flat sandy beaches, lush maritime forests, vast amounts of wildlife, and a rich variety of plant and marine life.

The region has long supported inhabitants—Native Americans, then English settlers, slaves, watermen, lighthouse keepers, members of the US Life-Saving Service, and many others who continue to shape the rich heritage of the Outer Banks. The people of the Outer Banks have witnessed storms, hurricanes, pirates, Civil War battles, hundreds of shipwrecks (including the USS *Monitor*), Billy Mitchell's test bombings, World War II, German U-boat attacks, secret military operations, Reginald Fessenden and the birth of radio broadcasts, and the mapping of the coast.

Congress officially authorized the Cape Hatteras National Seashore—the first national seashore park in the United States—on August 17, 1937. Three years later, the park was renamed the Cape Hatteras National Seashore Recreational Area to emphasize its intended purpose as a public seashore for everyone and anyone to enjoy. "Recreational Area" was dropped from the park's title in 1954. The establishment of the park led to the preservation of a significant portion of the "primitive wilderness" of the Outer Banks. The legislation also directed the National Park Service (NPS) to develop facilities for recreational beachgoers and to allow continued use of park resources by sport and commercial fishermen as well as hunters. During the seashore's creation, NPS also committed to combating the natural processes of shoreline erosion and accepted the development of roads along the entire length of the park.

The park was not actually established until January 1953. Key figures with great vision were unrelenting in their commitment to create, establish, and develop the seashore. The first of these figures was Frank Stick (1884–1966), an outdoorsman and commercial illustrator. Stick's involvement in real estate, however, was what positioned him to appreciate how development might affect the Outer Banks. Other key park supporters included North Carolina congressman Lindsay C. Warren (1891–1965), who sponsored the bill that sought to preserve the distinctive barrier islands of the Outer Banks, and his successor, Herbert C. Bonner, who continued to support the establishment of the park after Warren's term ended. Conrad L. Wirth (1899–1993), who became director of the National Park Service in 1953, was involved with Cape Hatteras from the early 1930s until the end of his directorship in 1964.

In 1930s and 1940s, travelling around the Cape Hatteras area required taking a flat-bottom metal tugboat across Oregon Inlet and then driving for miles across muddy and sandy "roads." Despite these dangerous conditions, hunters and fishermen made their way to the islands. While some locals became concerned about development, others donated or sold their parcels of oceanfront land (which, at the time, was not worth much), and the federal government purchased the rest.

The Works Progress Administration (WPA) and the Civilian Conservation Corps (CCC), public work relief programs that operated in the 1930s and 1940s as part of the New Deal, helped with projects along Cape Hatteras National Seashore. These included the construction of a dune line protecting the seashore from the encroaching ocean and miles of man-made dunes that created a barrier to protect both the villages and the sand roads. Some of these dunes are still standing today.

By the 1950s, Cape Hatteras National Seashore had become a more accessible beach vacation destination; the park was officially dedicated on April 24, 1958. A new beach house facility was constructed by the Cape Hatteras National Seashore on Coquina Beach in 1960.

The Bonner Bridge created an easy route across Oregon Inlet, and thousands of new visitors were able to access the seashore through the paved road now known as North Carolina Highway 12, which is now a National Scenic Byway. Development is limited to the town limits of Ocracoke Village and the seven villages on Hatteras Island, leaving miles of undeveloped shoreline wide open for visitors to explore. Because of this early planning, the Cape Hatteras National Seashore remains one of the largest and most visited stretches of wild, natural shorelines in the country.

The future of Cape Hatteras National Seashore will depend on local and state officials working together to protect the dynamic barrier islands of North Carolina's Outer Banks against the eroding forces of nature along the shoreline. Limited financial resources, continuing sea-level rise and climate change, and the long-term sustainability and preservation of historic structures and districts will continue to be a challenge. Public access to the beach is important to locals and visitors, but seasonal closures of certain beaches to vehicles, pedestrians, or both are required to protect threatened or endangered species as well as the shoreline.

In 2002, a team of North Carolina surveyors located a 6.75-mile baseline—small granite blocks marking each mile at Bodie Island, including two set by the US Coast Survey in 1848; the monuments are among the oldest surviving geodetic survey markers in the United States. The Hotel De Afrique, which no longer exists, was one of several lodgings where about 100 escaped slaves stayed after Union troops captured the Outer Banks early in the Civil War. A designation for the Hotel De Afrique was added to the National Underground Network to Freedom on July 31, 2013. Archeological artifacts and sites still remain under the sand within Cape Hatteras National Seashore for future generations to discover.

The historic photographs in this book cover the origins of Cape Hatteras National Seashore in the 1930s and progress through its main period of development under Mission 66 and into the 1970s. This will hopefully offer the reader a deeper understanding of the seashore's past.

One

ORIGINS OF A
PARK MOVEMENT

According to Cape Hatteras National Seashore historian Cameron Binkley, "In 1937, Conrad L. Wirth published an article entitled 'Cape Hatteras Seashore' in which he discussed how conservation work under National Park Service supervision had given a renewed impetus to the park and recreation movement in the United States. 'The American people,' wrote Wirth, 'are acquiring a new concept of outdoor recreation, and an appreciation of the value and importance of natural park areas. For that reason, and in line with its general policies, the Service is interested in the acquisition of certain natural, coastal areas to be set aside as national seashores where the people can get acquainted with and enjoy the beauty of the seacoast in its unspoiled state.'"

Frank Stick (seated) tours the waterways with other men from the hunting camp on Bodie Island. Stick—an outdoorsman, nature illustrator, conservationist, and real estate man—is credited with first popularizing the idea of creating a national coastal park in North Carolina. The North Carolina General Assembly created the Cape Hatteras Seashore Commission to acquire land for the proposed Cape Hatteras National Seashore, and Gov. Clyde R. Hoey appointed Stick as secretary of the commission. (Courtesy of Outer Banks History Center.)

Civilian Conservation Corps (CCC) boys prepare to cross Oregon Inlet in the 1930s at the same time Yellowstone superintendent Roger W. Toll led an NPS party to investigate the suitability of the Outer Banks as a national seashore in 1934. (Courtesy of Outer Banks History Center.)

This 1936 photograph shows South Bridge at New Inlet on Hatteras Island. This is the first movement of transportation and development of Cape Hatteras. On June 23, 1936, the National Park Service conduct a study "to gather data in developing a plan for coordinated and adequate public park, parkway, and recreational-area facilities development for the people of the United States" and assisted state and local governments in planning such facilities.

As shown in this 1936 image, automobile travel on the Outer Banks between Bodie Island and Ocracoke Islands was hazardous in the 1930s because vehicles had to maneuver through sand, mud, and water along the roadway.

Following a yearlong nationwide survey, the National Park Service recommended the preservation of 12 coastal areas as national seashores, with North Carolina's Outer Banks considered the most promising. Here, early park planners drive the sandy roads to survey the Hatteras seashore in 1936.

This seashore planner got stuck in the mud and water on Bodie Island in 1936. Automobile travel on the sandy roads and beaches of North Carolina's Outer Banks was often difficult for both vehicles and travelers.

This 1937 photograph shows the Cape Hatteras Lighthouse with sand fences in the foreground. Despite the use of fences and groins to forestall erosion, the ocean crept ever closer to the lighthouse. The tower, once a mile from the ocean, was only a few hundred feet from the waves in the mid-1930s. Consequently, the US Lighthouse Service abandoned the Cape Hatteras Lighthouse and extinguished the light on May 15, 1936. A year later, in 1937, Congress authorized the establishment of Cape Hatteras National Seashore. The envisioned park would stretch from the Virginia state line to Hatteras Inlet, encompassing some 62,000 acres. Its purpose was to preserve the area's "primitive wilderness" and to provide recreational access to the general public.

Pres. Franklin D. Roosevelt's New Deal included a beach erosion control and rehabilitation project on the Outer Banks, which brought thousands of men to work in the area under the leadership of A. Clark Stratton. This 1937 image shows Civilian Conservation Corps (CCC) men at Camp Diamond Shoals, located near Buxton, North Carolina; these men were assigned to work at Cape Hatteras.

Extra tents at Cape Hatteras Light Station accommodated workers from the Works Progress Administration (WPA) who assisted the CCC men at Diamond Shoals with constructing sand fences and planting beach grass.

This 1938 image shows Works Progress Administration (WPA) crews planting beach grass north of the old Phipps Gun Club near Buxton on Hatteras Island. The Cape Hatteras Lighthouse is visible in the background.

As shown in this 1938 photograph, Works Progress Administration (WPA) crews installed sand fences to encourage dune building along the Cape Hatteras shoreline. National Park Service officials grew concerned that erosion control projects might harm the future national seashore by removing too much vegetation. Between 1935 and 1941, the federal government spent several million dollars on erosion-control projects on the Outer Banks, putting unemployed men to work and preparing for the creation of a national seashore.

Two

DEVELOPMENT OF THE NATIONAL SEASHORE

This is the original Cape Hatteras National Seashore headquarters sign. Note that the park name is listed as "Cape Hatteras National Seashore Recreational Area." On June 29, 1940, Congress authorized legislation to permit hunting within the Cape Hatteras National Seashore, later defined in relationship to the Migratory Bird Treaty Act of 1918 to mean waterfowl hunting. "Recreational area" was added to the seashore's title in 1954 to emphasize the "recreational" orientation of the proposed seashore. With the formation of additional national seashores in the park system, the term "recreational area" was dropped, and seashores become known simply as "national seashores."

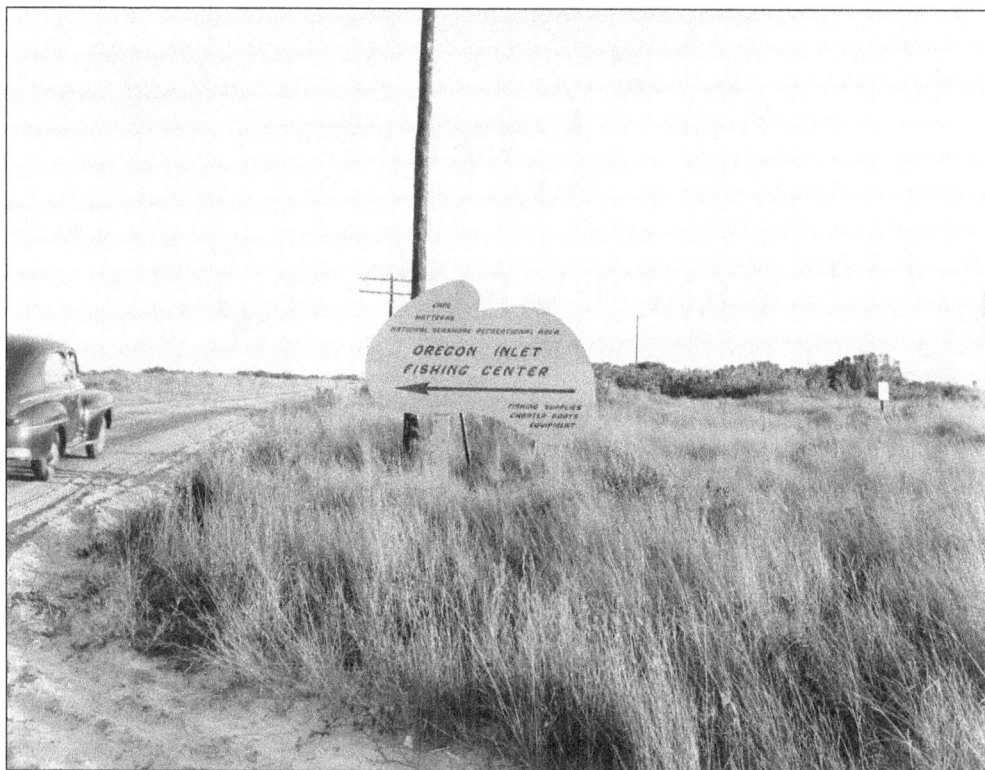

The National Park Service installed signs throughout the Cape Hatteras National Seashore in 1954. In the above image, a car is traveling north as it passes by the sign for the Oregon Inlet Fishing Marina within Cape Hatteras National Seashore. New highway signs (as shown below) also appeared along the Outer Banks within Cape Hatteras National Seashore.

This 1954 photograph looks south along the clay/gravel road leading to Oregon Inlet. Congress granted an easement to allow the state of North Carolina to construct and maintain a roadway through the Pea Island National Wildlife Refuge. Potential development increased the pressure to establish the national seashore.

The old road leading to the fishing center concession building is visible at right in this 1954 image showing new road construction near the Oregon Inlet Fishing Marina on Bodie Island.

This 1954 image looking north from the Oregon Inlet Fishing Marina concession building shows a new wooden retaining wall in the foreground and the current layout of shoreline and finger piers.

Control over the Oregon Inlet Fishing Marina, shown here in 1955 at the southern end of Bodie Island, was at the heart of the struggle to establish Cape Hatteras National Seashore.

These images from the Pirate's Jamboree held on Hatteras Island in 1955 show the display of flags extending from the gallery of the Cape Hatteras Lighthouse (above) and the crowd beginning to gather (below). The annual family event celebrates the maritime history of Ocracoke and Hatteras Island.

Here, a government truck surveys the new graded sandy road approaching Cape Hatteras Lighthouse in 1955.

This image shows the new graded road approaching the Cape Hatteras Light Station prior to hard surf in 1955.

These 1955 photographs show the construction of the Coquina Beach parking lot on Bodie Island. The Bodie Island Coast Guard Station and US Life-Saving Service Station are visible in the background of the above image.

The Coquina Beach parking lot is shown in 1956 complete with hard pavement. The Bodie Island Coast Guard Station and US Life-Saving Service Station are visible in the background.

In 1956, sandy roads were resurfaced with hard pavement north of Oregon Inlet on Bodie Island. Note the large sand dunes intended to protect the road.

Beach grass, pictured near Pea Island in 1956, was planted on the dunes in an effort to control erosion and protect the new paved highway through the seashore.

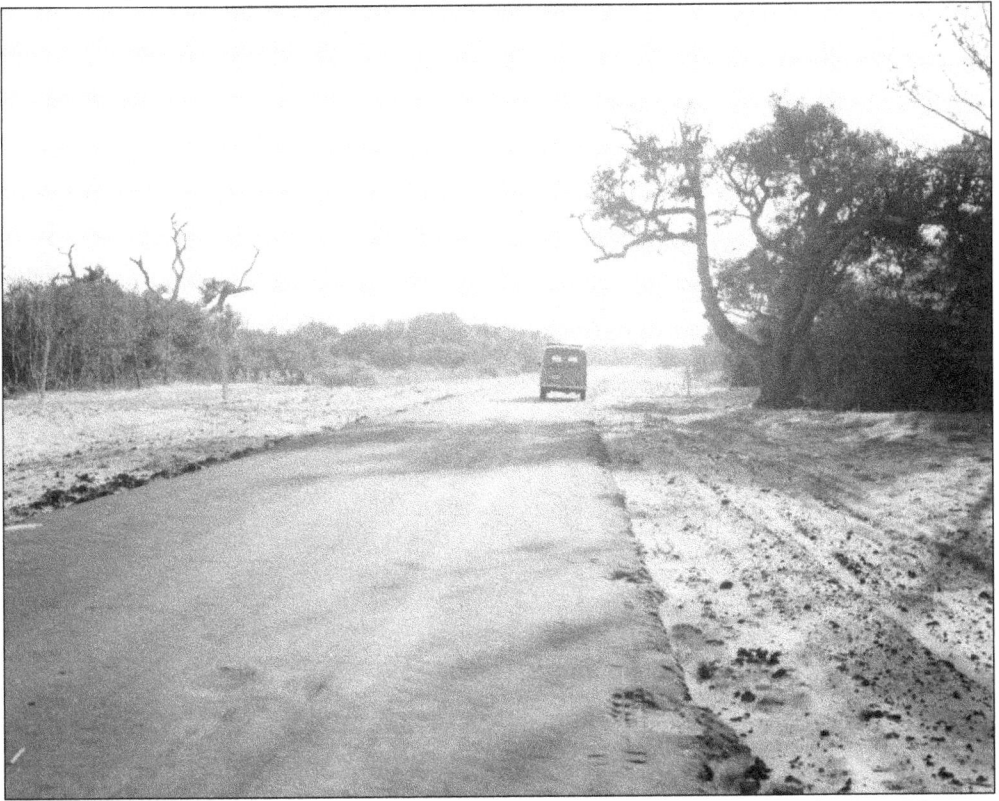

A government vehicle drives along the new hard road surface from Buxton to the Cape Hatteras Lighthouse area. Old live oak trees are protected along the roadway.

Above, cattle stand on the beach near the remains of the Carol A. Deering shipwreck on Ocracoke Island. Wild ponies and livestock grazed freely on the seashore during the National Park Service–led erosion-control projects. Below, a government vehicle is parked on the beach with livestock in the background at Ocracoke Island in 1956.

Ponies graze near the Pamlico Sound on Ocracoke Island in 1956. The Ocracoke ponies are believed to be descended from Spanish horses. In September 2014, there were 16 full-time residents at the pony pens on Ocracoke Island, a fenced complex that includes 180 acres of pasture. The National Park Service fenced in the ponies for protection after the paved North Carolina Highway 12 was built on Ocracoke; the pens also prevent the ponies from overgrazing the island's vegetation.

The Ocracoke "Banker" ponies are pictured here in a pen adjacent to the Sam Jones Berkley Manor in the village of Ocracoke. This photograph was taken from the tower room of the manor house during pony-penning activities in 1956.

This sunrise service was held at Cape Hatteras Lighthouse in 1956.

The North Carolina State Ferry System began transporting locals and visitors across Hatteras Inlet between Hatteras and Ocracoke Island in the mid-1920s. This image shows vehicles being loaded onto the ferry at Hatteras Village in 1957.

These images show Sen. Roman L. Hruska, of Nebraska, casting a line at Cape Hatteras National Seashore in 1957. Above, Hruska stands with District Park Ranger Charles Lamb (right); at right, Hruska is pictured with local author and journalist Ben Dixon McNeil (far right).

Victoria Hruska, wife of Nebraska senator Roman L. Hruska, fishes in the surf at Cape Hatteras National Seashore in 1957.

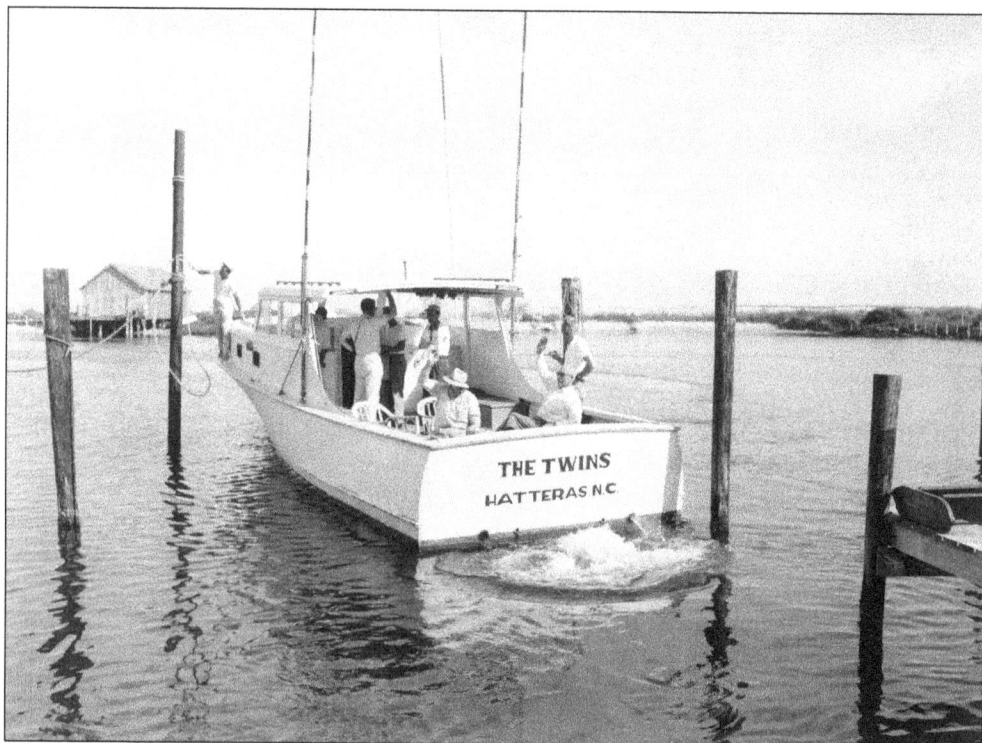

A charter fishing boat heads for the Gulf Stream from the Hatteras Blue Marlin dock. Aboard are North Carolina governor Clyde R. Hoey and some friends for a day of fishing off the coast of Hatteras in 1957.

The North Carolina General Assembly created the Cape Hatteras Seashore Commission to acquire land for the proposed location of Cape Hatteras National Seashore. On December 22, 1952, the Cape Hatteras Seashore Commission recommended that Gov. William Kerr Scott transfer several thousand acres of state-owned lands in Dare and Hyde Counties to create the national seashore. Governor Scott formally conveyed the property to the federal government. The commissioners pictured here in 1957 are, from left to right, Maurice Burrus, Woodrow Price, Gen. Don Scott, Mrs. Roland McClamroch, Carlton Kelly, Conrad L. Wirth, George R. Ross, E.M. Lisle, Thomas W. Morse, Elbert Cox, A.C. Stratton, and three unidentified.

Allyn F. Hanks (pictured) served as the first superintendent of Cape Hatteras National Seashore from 1954 to 1957. The first permanent National Park Service personnel arrived at the seashore for duty as the park continued to develop.

National Park Service director Conrad L. Wirth attended this potluck dinner at the Bodie Island Visitor Center in 1957. Pictured here are, from left to right, Helen Hanks, wife of park superintendent Allyn F. Hanks; Wirth; Lucile Lamb; Louise Meekins; ? Hall; and Peg Watson.

Florence Taffeta, from the National Park Service Office of Chief, Public Information Section, tours and gathers information at Cape Hatteras National Seashore in 1957.

Cape Hatteras National Seashore's first constructed restroom station was located at the Bodie Island parking area in 1957.

10 View South from Bath House
Coquina Beach

This image shows the bathhouse under construction at Coquina Beach on March 13, 1956. The National Park Service awarded a construction contract for the Coquina Beach facilities to Daniels Building Supply and Shanaberger Lumber Company of Nags Head. The project was completed in October 1956.

Pictured in 1957 is Cape Hatteras National Seashore's first bathhouse at Coquina Beach on Bodie Island after its construction. The structure was a modern architectural design for the seashore.

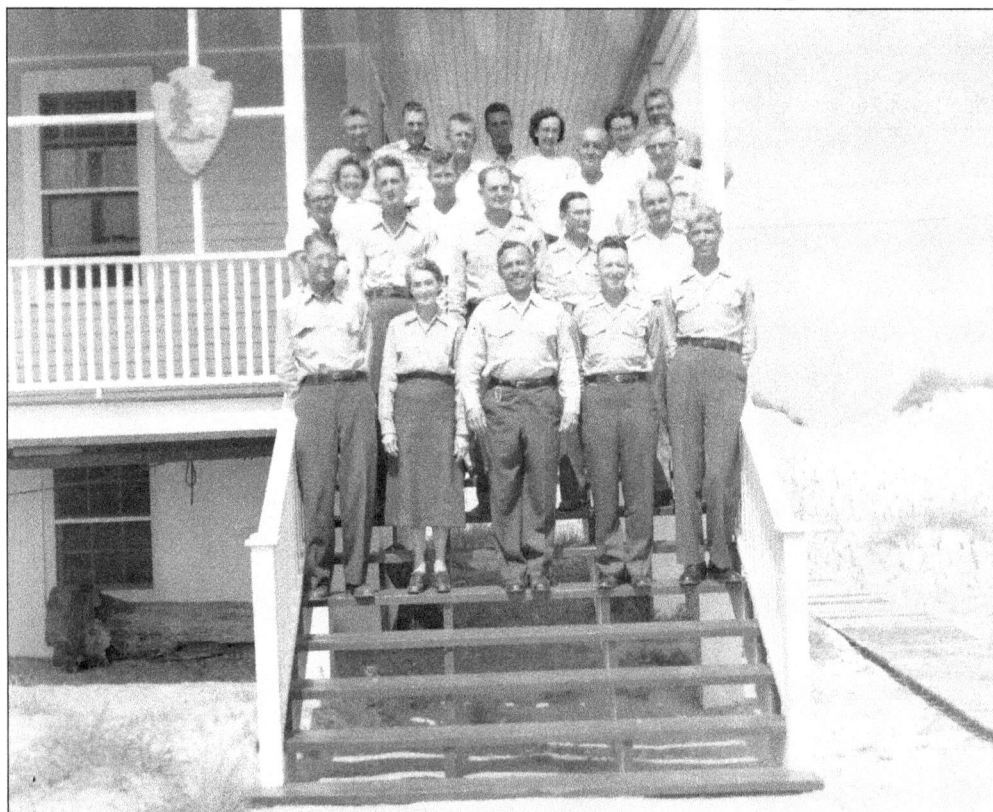

The national seashore's employees are pictured at the park headquarters at the old Bodie Island Coast Guard Station in September 1957. From left to right are (first row) Balfour Baum (supervisory park ranger), Louise Meekins (tour leader), Allyn Hanks (superintendent), Verde Watson (park naturalist), and Gus Hultman (chief park ranger). The rest are unidentified.

34

Three

ESTABLISHMENT OF THE
NATIONAL SEASHORE

This photograph shows the Cape Hatteras Lighthouse at Cape Hatteras National Seashore. According to historian Cameron Binkley, "The Cape Hatteras Lighthouse towers over Diamond Shoals at Cape Hatteras National Seashore. Charles Marshall, Cape Hatteras project manager, reported that 24,705 of 28,500 acres along the seashore were under federal ownership. Congress approved a provision transferring some 43 acres of federal land in the village of Hatteras to the national seashore without any exchange of funds to benefit a local nonprofit. The seashore's dedication ceremonies were held at Coquina Beach and at the Cape Hatteras Lighthouse on April 24, 1958."

Dedication Program

Cape Hatteras

National Seashore Recreational Area

COQUINA BEACH ON
BODIE ISLAND

and

CAPE HATTERAS
LIGHTHOUSE

HATTERAS ISLAND

NATIONAL
PARK
SERVICE

Department
of the Interior

APRIL 24, 1958

UNITED STATES
DEPARTMENT OF
THE INTERIOR

Cape Hatteras Lighthouse

This is the front of the official program from the dedication of the Cape Hatteras National Seashore Recreational Area, which was held on April 24, 1958, at Coquina Beach on Bodie Island and at the Cape Hatteras Lighthouse on Hatteras Island.

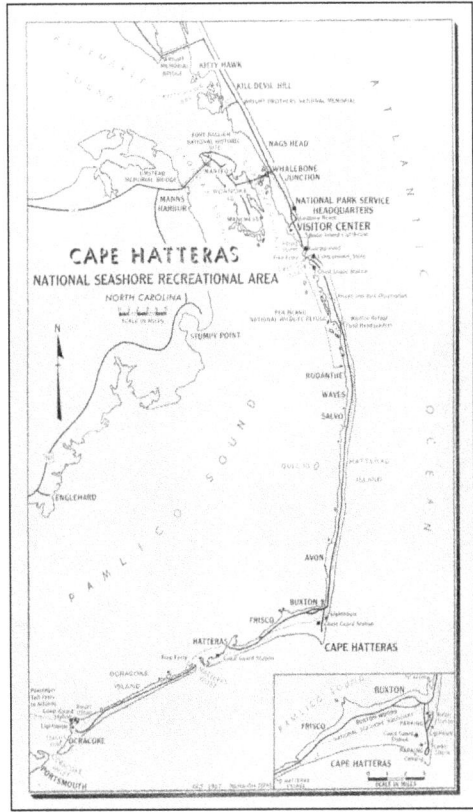

A park map (right) and the order of ceremonies (below) were included in the official dedication program for the Cape Hatteras National Seashore Recreational Area.

CAPE HATTERAS
NATIONAL SEASHORE RECREATIONAL AREA
NORTH CAROLINA

PROGRAM

11:30 A.M.

Presiding	Mr. Conrad L. Wirth
	Director National Park Service
Invocation	The Reverend L. R. Sparrow
	The Hatteras Methodist Charge
Introductions	Mr. Conrad L. Wirth
Unveiling Ceremony	Mr. Raymond R. Guest

Unveiling of Bronze Plaque commemorating the gift of 2700 acres of land by the family of Henry Phipps to the Cape Hatteras National Seashore.

OCRACOKE LIGHTHOUSE AND KEEPER'S QUARTERS

PROGRAM

2:30 P.M.

Presiding	Mr. Conrad L. Wirth
	Director National Park Service
Musical Selection	The National Anthem
	Elizabeth City High School Band
	Mr. Scott C. Calloway, Director
Invocation	The Reverend Robert Turner
	Pastor St. Andrews By-The-Sea
	Episcopal Church
Introductions	Mr. Conrad L. Wirth
Greetings	Mr. Lindsay Warren
	Mr. Paul Mellon
	The Honorable
	Governor Luther H. Hodges
Dedication Address	Mr. Roger C. Ernst
	Assistant
	Secretary of the Interior
Special Ceremony	

Mixing waters of Yellowstone, the first National Park, with waters of Cape Hatteras, the first National Seashore.

The Honorable
Governor Luther H. Hodges
Mr. Roger C. Ernst
Mr. Lindsay Warren
Rear Admiral
H. C. Moore, U.S.C.G.
Robert F. Gibbs, Superintendent

Coronation	The Honorable
	Luther H. Hodges

Crowning the Pirates Jamboree King and Queen

America The Beautiful
Elizabeth City High School Band

Many dignitaries gathered for the dedication ceremonies at Cape Hatteras National Seashore, which was held on April 24, 1958, at Coquina Beach on Bodie Island. Pictured above are, from left to right, Assistant Secretary of the Interior Roger C. Ernst, Congressmen Herbert C. Bonner, National Park Service director Conrad L. Wirth, Paul Mellon, Gov. Luther Hodges, Congressman Lindsay Warren, and three other unidentified congressmen. Below, Bonner is shown speaking at the dedication for the Cape Hatteras National Seashore on April 24, 1958.

Actor Andy Griffith—who had his roots and a home in the Outer Banks—spoke at the dedication ceremony for Cape Hatteras National Seashore on April 24, 1958, at Coquina Beach on Bodie Island.

Park superintendent Robert F. Gibbs (left) and US Coast Guard rear admiral H.C. Moore (right) are shown "mixing the waters" from the Old Faithful geyser (located in Yellowstone National Park) and the Atlantic Ocean during the dedication ceremony for the Cape Hatteras National Seashore on April 24, 1958. Yellowstone was the first national park and Cape Hatteras National Seashore was the first national seashore dedicated under the National Park Service.

North Carolina governor Luther Hodges is shown crowning the Jamboree queen following the Cape Hatteras National Seashore dedication ceremony on April 24, 1958, at Coquina Beach on Bodie Island.

The National Park Service chartered this Trailways bus to transport dignitaries from Bodie Island to Hatteras Island and Oregon Inlet on the ferry en route to the Phipps Plaque dedication ceremonies on April 24, 1958, at the Cape Hatteras Lighthouse.

The Phipps Plaque dedication ceremony—commemorating the family of Henry Phipps for their gift of approximately 2,700 acres of land to Cape Hatteras National Seashore—was held on April 24, 1958, at Cape Hatteras Lighthouse. Below, Raymond Guest (left) and Gov. Luther H. Hodges (right) unveil the plaque.

These 1958 images show the construction of a new state highway that bypasses South Nags Head Road (the old North Carolina State Route 12) through Whalebone Junction to become the new north entrance to the seashore on Bodie Island.

Park maintenance erects a fence to rebuild dunes at Cape Hatteras National Seashore after Hurricane Helene on September 27, 1958. Cape Hatteras sustained 100 mile-per-hour winds, which tore up the new roads and destroyed 75 percent of the dune stabilization work completed on Ocracoke Island at the time.

Workers are shown preparing to erect fencing for dune building. On September 11, 1960, Hurricane Donna slammed into the Outer Banks with winds up to 123 miles per hour, causing extensive damage to the dune system on Ocracoke Island. There was also scattered damage to dunes, buildings, roads, walkways, and vegetation throughout the seashore.

Tractor-driven mechanical grass planters assisted park maintenance with replanting beach grass throughout the park on Ocracoke Island in 1960.

Park maintenance erected sand fencing to encourage dune building near the Cape Hatteras Lighthouse in 1960.

In 1960, park maintenance replanted beach grass on Bodie Island (above) and spread fertilizer by helicopter (below) on newly planted beach grass throughout the seashore.

These 1960 images show park maintenance crews installing beach ramps to access the beach and prevent vehicles from driving over the sand dunes (left) and repairing a beach ramp after a storm washed away the dune (below).

This ramp, pictured in 1960, offered access to the beach over a sand dune.

An unidentified park ranger investigates damage at Ramp 8, located north of Rodanthe, in 1960.

The seashore has two inlets, Oregon Inlet on Bodie Island and Hatteras Inlet in Hatteras. Here, visitors lined up to wait for the Hatteras Inlet Ferry at a slip south of Hatteras Village in 1960.

Vehicles lined up to await the arrival of the Oregon Inlet Ferry at the south slip in 1960. More than 100 vehicles are in this line, which extends around the bend behind the camera.

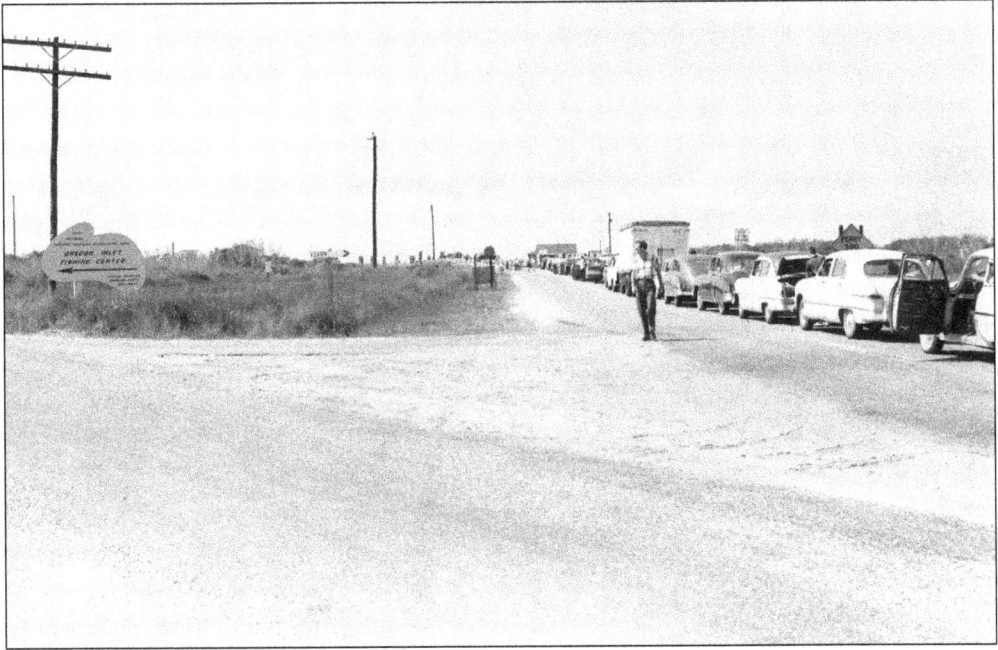

Both of these 1960 images show visitors lined up while waiting for the Oregon Inlet Ferry.

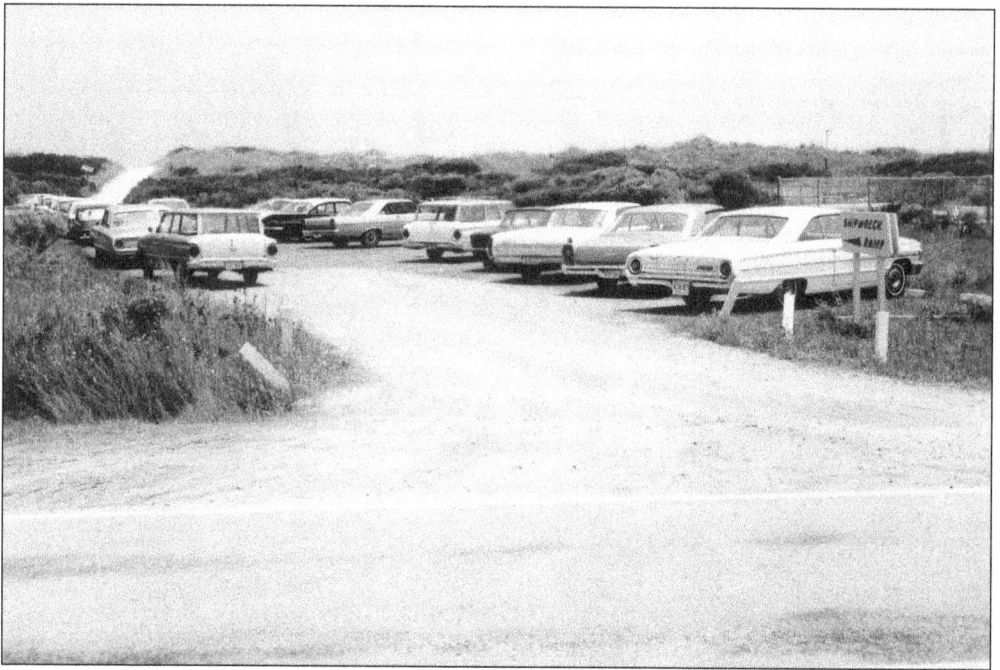

Overcrowded parking areas became a problem along the seashore. These 1960 images show cars filling a parking lot near the Laura Barnes Shipwreck on Bodie Island (above) and an overcrowded boat launching area at Oregon Inlet Fishing Marina over the Fourth of July weekend (below).

In these 1960 images, small-boat operators launch from inadequate facilities adjacent to the Oregon Inlet Fishing Marina.

The above image shows the newly constructed 1960 Bodie Island Park Maintenance Building. The image below shows the 1950 Bodie Island Park Maintenance Building near the Bodie Island Lighthouse. Both structures are still used today.

The Billy Mitchell Airport—constructed in Frisco, North Carolina, in 1960—allowed private planes to land and park while visiting the seashore. The airstrip is still managed by the State of North Carolina and under a permit from Cape Hatteras National Seashore. The image below shows a British ambassador arriving at the Billy Mitchell Airport in 1961.

The Coquina Beach facility at Bodie Island is pictured above sometime in 1960 and below on July 4, 1960. The Coquina Beach facility is part of the National Park Service's Mission 66 program, a decade-long effort to improve the visitor experience through construction of new facilities in national parks during the mid-20th century.

Park visitors picnicked under the Coquina Beach facility shade structure (above) and used the outdoor showers (below) at Bodie Island during the Fourth of July weekend in 1960.

Park visitors used the facilities and picnicked at Coquina Beach on Bodie Island in 1960.

One of the newly built comfort stations in the Cape Hatteras Campground is pictured here in 1961.

This checking station for wild fowl hunting was located about a mile and a half south of Whalebone Junction in 1961. Seashore superintendent Robert F. Gibbs issued hunting regulations on September 10, 1958, per the authorizing legislation and agreements with the local community.

Pictured at left is the entrance station to the Oregon Inlet Campground in 1961. It was replaced with the new structure below in 1965.

Park rangers check on campers at Ocracoke Campground in 1961.

Campgrounds on the beach were inundated with ocean water in 1961.

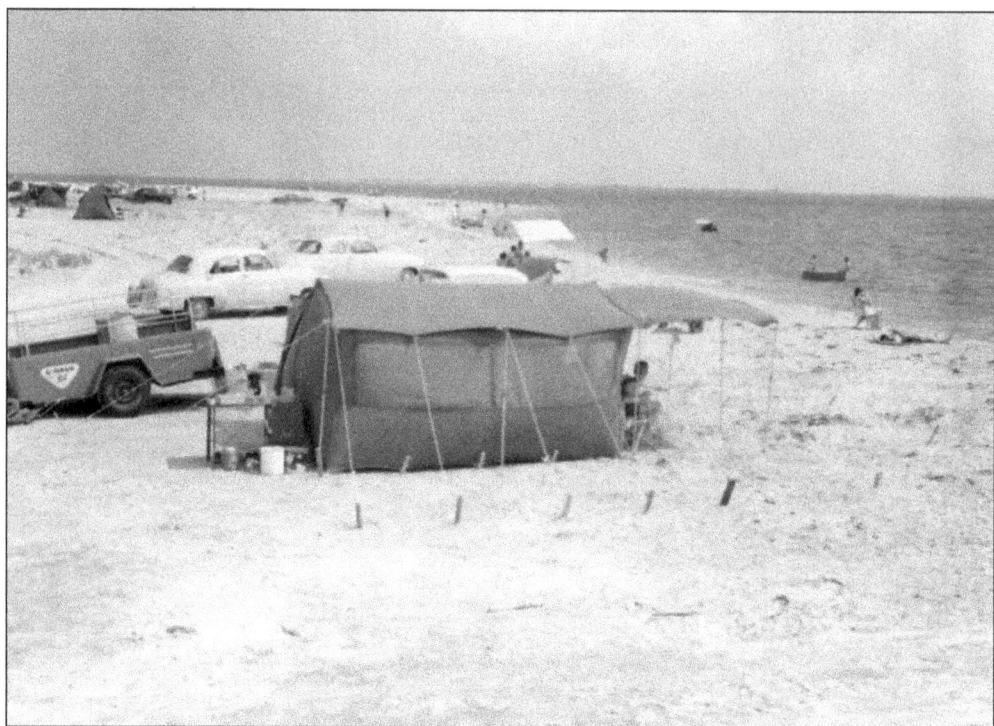

The campers in these 1961 photographs are just north of North Point (above) and at Oregon Inlet (below).

These 1961 images show campers at Cape Hatteras Campground (above) and Ocracoke Oceanside Campground (below).

A seasonal park ranger shows a map of the Cape Hatteras National Seashore to park visitors at Bodie Island Visitor Center in 1962. Mission 66 envisioned major interpretative improvements, including a modern visitor center.

A park ranger talks to children about birds of the Outer Banks at the Bodie Island Visitor Center in 1962.

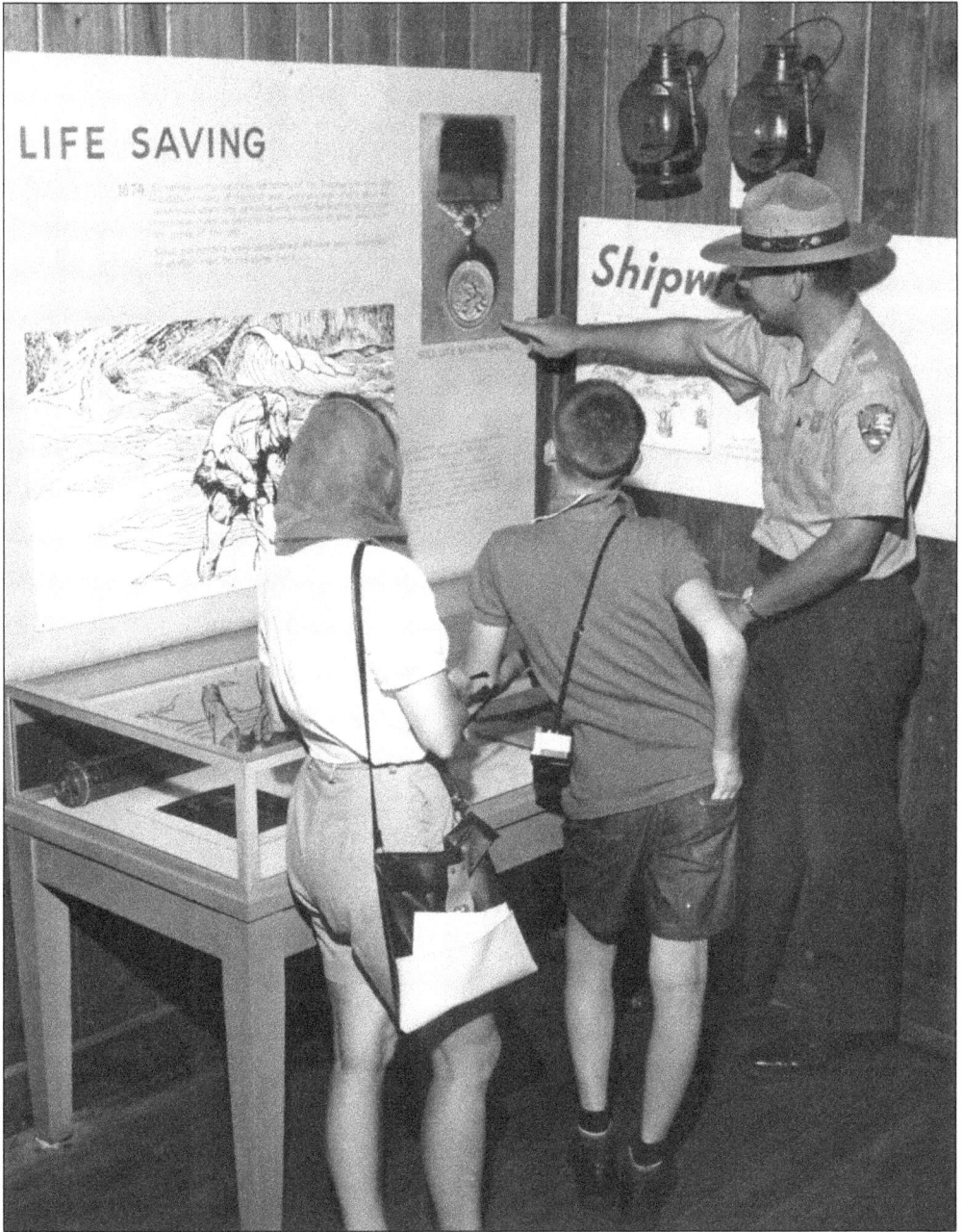

In this 1962 photograph, a seasonal park ranger talks to park visitors at the Museum of the Sea (located in the former double keepers' quarters at the Cape Hatteras Light Station) about a US Life-Saving Service Gold Medal given to a life-saver after a rescue.

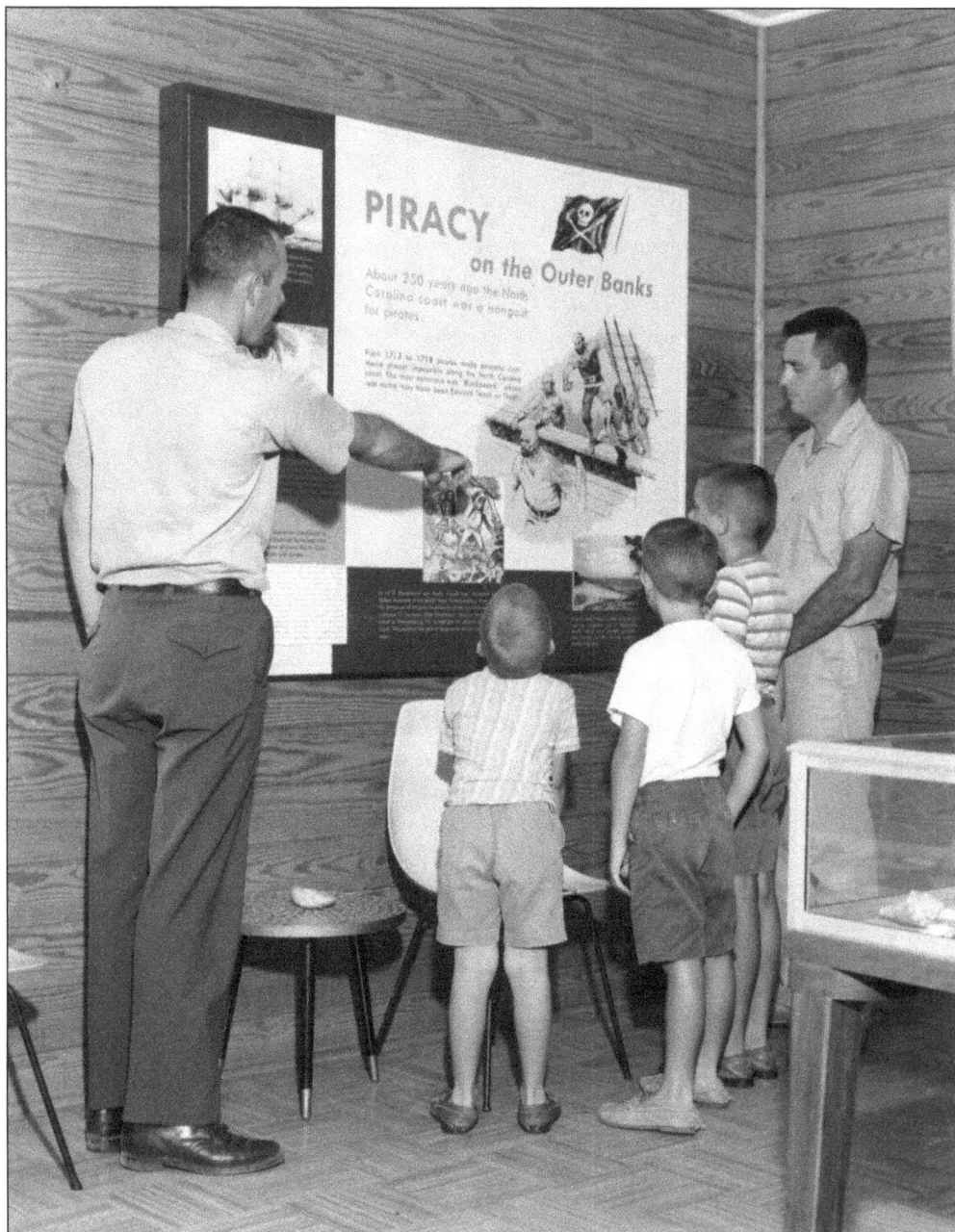

A seasonal park ranger discusses piracy with park visitors at the Ocracoke Island Visitor Center in 1963.

Above, a seasonal park ranger shows park visitors a collection of US Weather Bureau lanterns at the Museum of the Sea in 1963. Below, district naturalist Clay Gifford gives a talk on the porch at the Museum of the Sea in 1963.

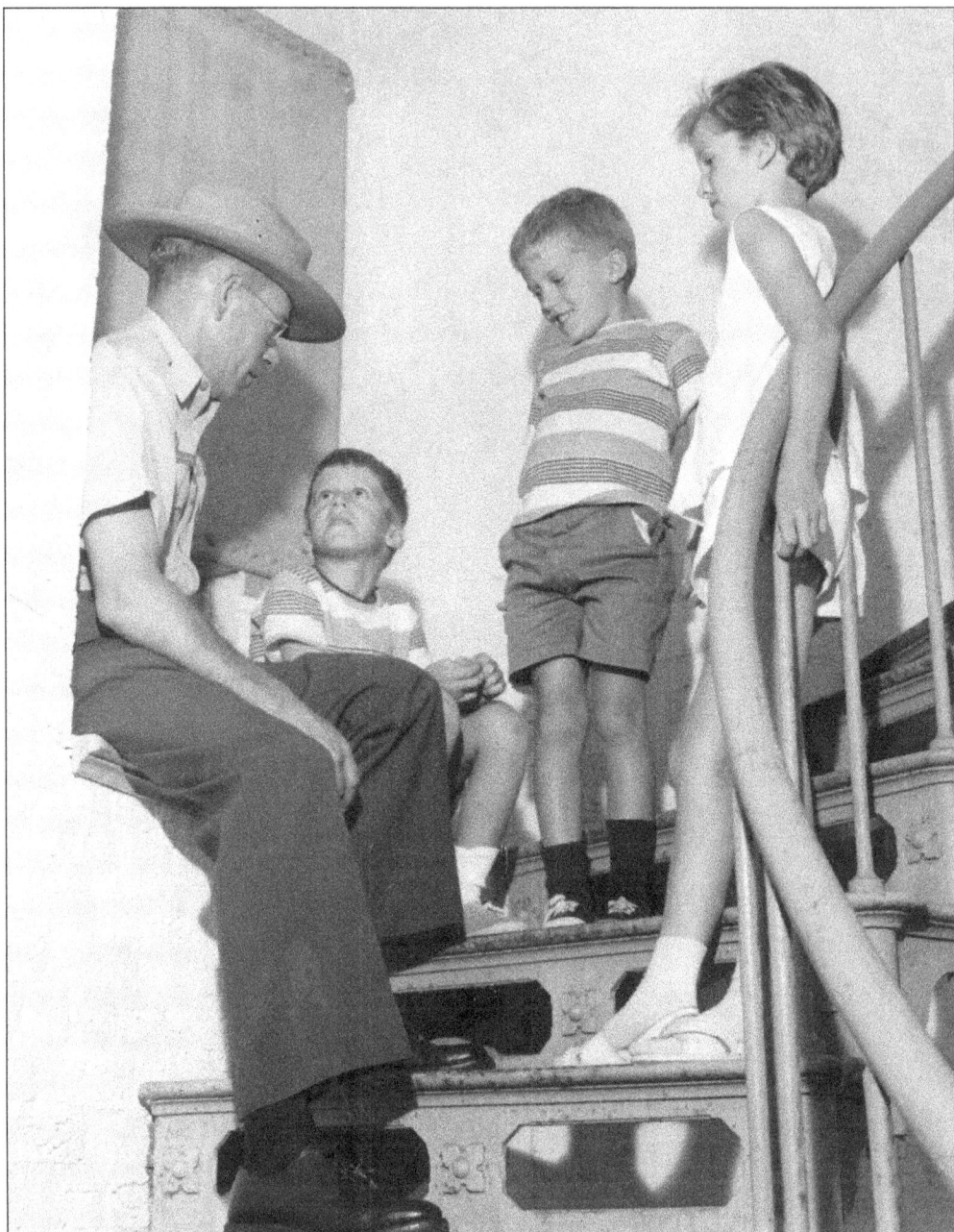

District naturalist Clay Gifford talks with children inside the Cape Hatteras Lighthouse in 1963.

Park visitors begin a beach walk with district naturalist Clay Gifford at the Cape Hatteras Lighthouse in 1963.

Seasonal naturalist Jerry Stone talks with a group of visitors on the observation platform behind the Bodie Island Lighthouse in 1963.

A seasonal naturalist talks with a group of park visitors on the beach at the seashore in 1963.

The Herbert C. Bonner Bridge was constructed across Oregon Inlet to allow visitors to travel within Cape Hatteras National Seashore. Congress authorized the Department of the Interior to contribute $500,000 toward the cost of constructing the bridge. North Carolina congressman Herbert C. Bonner was the main force behind passage of this bill. As a memento, Pres. John F. Kennedy gave Bonner the pen he had used to sign the bill. Construction of the bridge over Oregon Inlet took approximately two years and had a huge impact on village life on Hatteras Island.

North Carolina governor Terry Sanford dedicated the Herbert C. Bonner Bridge on May 2, 1964. The new bridge was the first ever built between Hatteras and Bodie Islands.

This 1964 photograph offers an aerial view of Bodie Island and the Oregon Inlet Campground (center), the Oregon Inlet Fishing Marina (right), and the new Herbert C. Bonner Bridge (background).

This 1964 aerial view shows the Oregon Inlet Fishing Marina and the Oregon Inlet Campground at the southern end of Bodie Island.

This is a 1964 aerial view of the Hatteras Inlet Coast Guard Station (left), located on the southern end of Hatteras Island within the Cape Hatteras National Seashore. Constructed in 1962, the station is situated on six acres of National Park Service land. Visitors traveling between Hatteras and Ocracoke Island could board ferries at the Hatteras Ferry Dock.

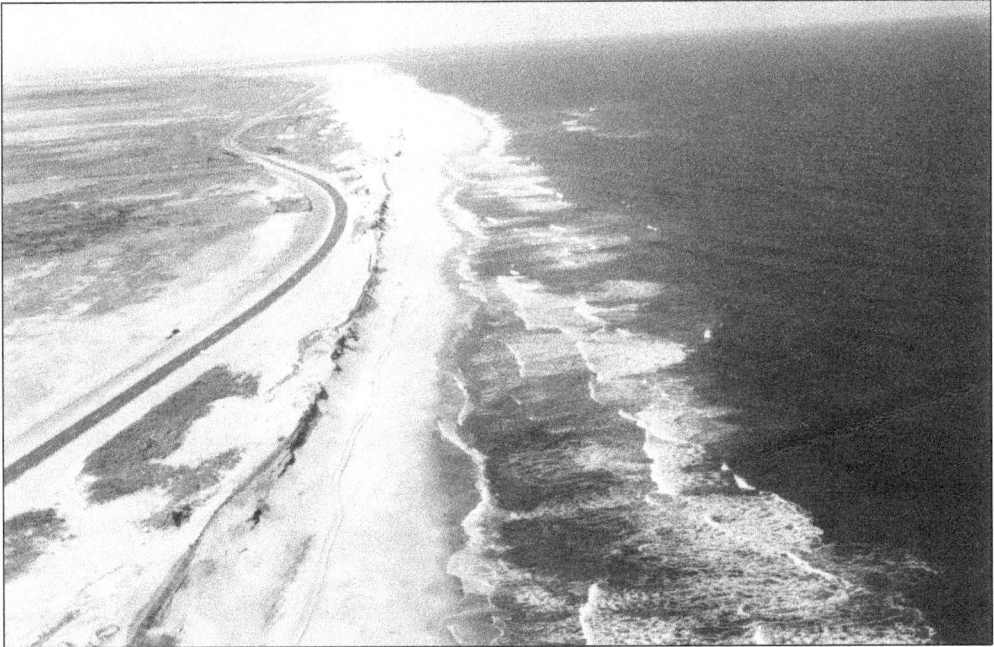

This 1964 aerial image shows the new S-curved road and looks north from the village of Rodanthe. The road was damaged during a storm, which caused the relocation of North Carolina Highway 12. Ocean water continues to be an ongoing issue with highway maintenance.

The construction and operation of fishing piers at Frisco and Rodanthe (one pictured here in 1965) raised concerns of National Park Service construction oversight during the development of the seashore.

In February 1956, the National Park Service issued a request for proposals to construct, maintain, and operate one or more ocean piers, which drew much criticism in Dare County over the National Park Service having control over operations of the piers. This 1972 photograph shows the Rodanthe Pier.

Four

NATURAL AND CULTURAL PARK RESOURCES

Cape Hatteras National Seashore contains a wealth of natural and cultural resources. The seashore provides habitat for a host of plants and wildlife, while cultural resources like the Cape Hatteras Lighthouse draw visitors from around the world. Preserving the seashore's resources remains the park's most important mission.

Surf fishing at Cape Hatteras National Seashore, as shown in this 1960 photograph, offers anglers a variety of excellent opportunities and is one of many recreational activities available to seashore visitors. The success of Cape Hatteras National Seashore was a model for future coastal parks.

This 1956 photograph shows "haul netters" fishing for rockfish at Cape Hatteras National Seashore.

These fishermen are shown on the boat *Jackie Fay* at Cape Hatteras on December 10, 1952. Outer Bankers faced an uncertain future as change threatened their traditional lifestyle in the mid-20th century. Most saw tourism as the way forward, but park opponents championed private property rights over public ownership and conservation.

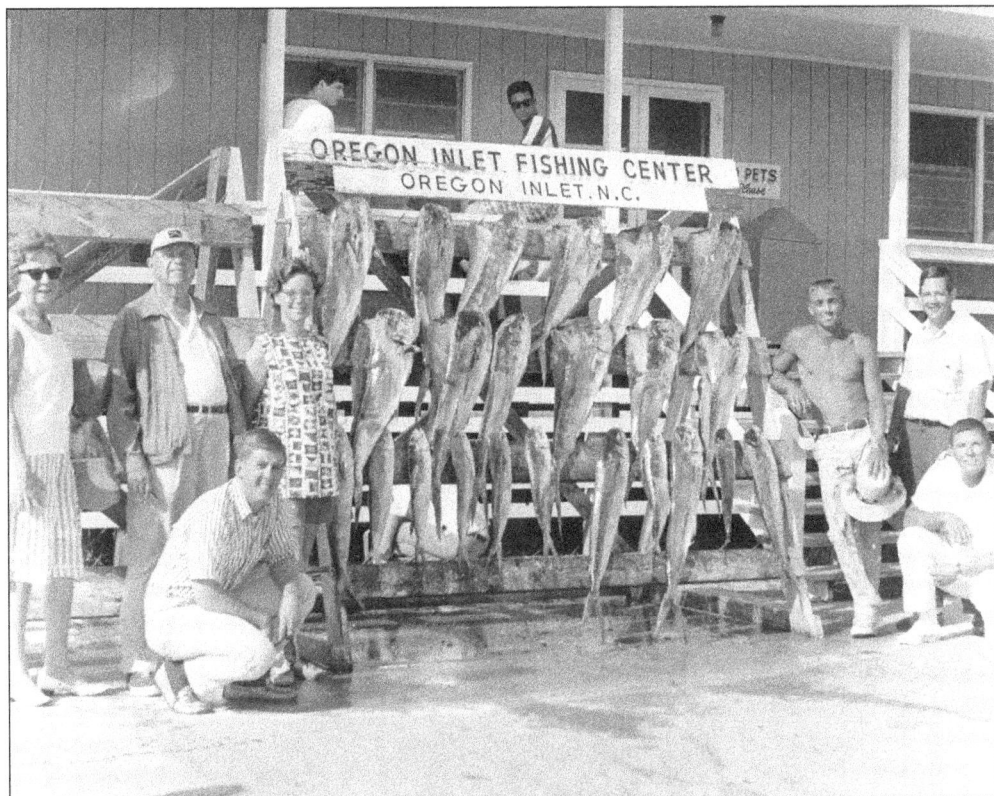

The catch of the day is displayed at the Oregon Inlet Fishing Marina, located within Cape Hatteras National Seashore, in 1970. Fishing along Cape Hatteras National Seashore is phenomenal due to its close proximity to the Gulf Stream and the Labrador Current.

This 300-pound leatherback turtle washed ashore near Coquina Beach in 1970.

An unidentified visitor poses with a dead dolphin that washed ashore on Hatteras Island in 1973.

These two finback whales washed ashore on Hatteras Island in 1971.

A flock of snow geese on Bodie Island take flight in 1971. Nearly 400 species of birds have been sighted within Cape Hatteras National Seashore and its surrounding waters. This impressive number is due to several factors: a location on the Atlantic Flyway, varied habitats, and strong winds and storms that often bring exhausted vagrants to the area's shores.

The 1965 image above shows an aerial view of the Bodie Island Lighthouse, ponds, and the Atlantic Ocean. The Bodie Island Lighthouse is correctly called a light station because a light station comprises the lighthouse tower and all outbuildings, such as the keeper's living quarters and oil houses. Below is a 1965 aerial view of the Bodie Island Light Station from Pamlico Sound, a private hunting camp accessible by boat, which is visible on the lower left side of the picture.

This 1965 aerial view of Cape Hatteras National Seashore shows the first bathhouse at Coquina Beach and the Bodie Island Lighthouse and ponds in the background.

The Bodie Island Lighthouse (pictured in 1964) underwent a three-year, $5-million restoration in 2012. The 1872 Bodie Island Lighthouse is now open for visitors who want to climb the 214 steps that spiral to the top. The 156-foot structure is one of only a dozen remaining brick tower lighthouses in the United States and one of the few with an original first-order Fresnel lens to cast its light. The restored double keepers' quarters houses a visitor center and a bookstore.

This 1964 image shows the Bodie Island Lighthouse and keeper's dwelling. The Bodie Island Light Station is listed in the National Register of Historic Places. The current Bodie Island Lighthouse is the third that has stood in this vicinity along the Outer Banks and was built in 1872 and automated in 1940. The current tower is 156 feet tall with a focal plane of 156 feet above sea level.

The Bodie Island Lighthouse (pictured in 1960) contains a beautiful first-order Fresnel lens that casts its beacon 19 nautical miles out into the Atlantic Ocean. There are 214 cast-iron steps from the base to the top of the tower. In July 2000, the Bodie Island Lighthouse was officially transferred from the US Coast Guard to the National Park Service. On April 25, 2005, the USCG transferred the title of the first-order Fresnel lens to the National Park Service, and the lens is now classified as a private aid to navigation.

The Bodie Island Lighthouse and keeper's dwelling are shown here in 1957. It is interesting to note that some people refer to the name as "Bodie" with a long "o," while others refer to it using the same pronunciation as the word "body." "Body" is the recommended pronunciation by locals. It is believed that the reason for this is because the tract of land that the light sits on was originally purchased from the Body family. Another theory suggests that it was named for a "body of land."

The Bodie Island Light Station (pictured in 1956) was completed in 1872. Light keepers lived on this isolated island to keep the beacon lit, carrying oil up the spiral stairs twice each day. The keeper's quarters were extensively remodeled in the 1970s to provide the National Park Service with offices on the second floor and an interpretive center and gift shop on the first floor.

This is a 1956 view southwest from the Bodie Island Lighthouse gallery deck. The view from the top of the lighthouse provides a stunning 360-degree panorama that not only includes the pristine marshland that makes up the southern end of Bodie Island, but also an uninterrupted vista of the Atlantic Ocean, Oregon Inlet, and Roanoke and Pamlico Sounds.

This photograph of the new parking lot, as viewed from the Bodie Island Lighthouse gallery deck, was taken in 1956.

The Bodie Island Light Station keepers' quarters shows signs of neglect and abandonment in this 1954 photograph. The Bodie Island Lighthouse was built north of Oregon Inlet on 15 acres of property purchased for $150 from John Etheridge. Work crews, equipment, and materials from the recent lighthouse project at Cape Hatteras were used to build necessary loading docks, dwellings, and facilities. Government contracts brought bricks and stone from Baltimore firms and ironwork from a New York foundry.

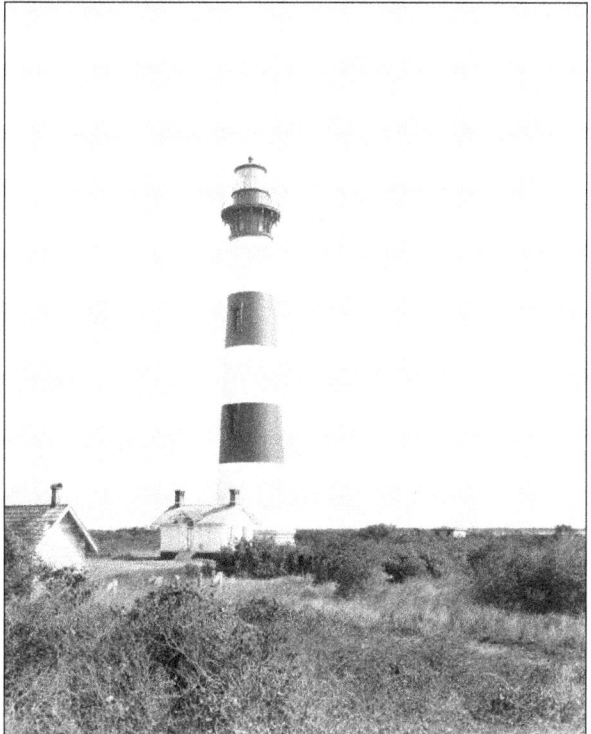

In the 1954 image at right, the Bodie Island Lighthouse is overgrown with vegetation.

The Cape Hatteras Lighthouse, built in 1870 (pictured in 1974) with its black and white candy cane stripes, is one of the most famous and recognizable lighthouses in the world. In 1867, Congress appropriated the necessary funds, and construction was begun in 1868. At $155,000, the second and present Cape Hatteras Light was one of the more expensive lights on the East Coast. The lighthouse contains approximately 1,250,000 bricks, which came from various brick kilns along the James River in Virginia. Dexter Stetson was the superintendent of construction. The lighthouse protects seagoing vessels from one of the most hazardous sections of the Atlantic Coast. Offshore from Cape Hatteras, the Gulf Stream collides with the Labrador Current from Canada. These currents force southbound ships into a dangerous 12-mile-long sandbar called Diamond Shoals.

In 1999, the 4,400-ton Cape Hatteras Lighthouse (pictured in 1974) was successfully relocated 2,900 feet from the location where it had stood since 1870. Because of the threat of shoreline erosion, the entire light station was safely moved to a new site, where the historic buildings and cisterns were placed in spatial and elevational relationship to each other exactly as they had been at the original site.

The Cape Hatteras Lighthouse went into commission on December 1, 1870. Constructed on an octagonal "floating foundation" of pine timbers and granite layers, its height—198.49 feet from the ground to the top of the lightning rod—makes it the tallest brick lighthouse in the United States. Its characteristic black-and-white spiral-striped paint pattern is clearly shown in this 1970 photograph.

In March 1980, a winter storm swept away the remnants of the 1803 lighthouse foundation (shown on the right in this 1970 image) and caused significant dune erosion. On November 9, 1937, the Cape Hatteras Light Station was transferred to the National Park Service. While the park was not operational at the time, the lighthouse and the keepers' quarters became part of the nation's first national seashore. In 1950, when the structure was again found safe for use, new lighting equipment was installed. The Coast Guard now owns and operates the navigational equipment, while the National Park Service maintains the tower as a historic structure.

The 10-acre Cape Hatteras Light Station Historic District was listed in the National Register of Historic Places in 1978. Following the successful relocation of the light station in 1999, it was designated a National Historic Landmark and classified as a Civil Engineering Landmark. This photograph was taken in 1965.

In addition to the lighthouse, supporting structures—including the oil house and both the principal and assistant keeper's dwellings—comprise the Cape Hatteras Light Station, which is pictured here in 1956.

Visitors on the Cape Hatteras Lighthouse balcony enjoy the view of Cape Point in the 1955 photograph above; below is a US Navy facility once located north of the Cape Hatteras Lighthouse, as shown in a photograph taken from the lighthouse's balcony in 1955.

This 1955 image shows coastal erosion at the Cape Hatteras Lighthouse. In 1966, the National Park Service (NPS) pumped 312,000 cubic yards of sand ashore, but it later disappeared. A year later, large sandbags placed on the shore by NPS did little to help. In 1969, more steel groins were put in place in an attempt to capture sand. Between 1971 and 1973, a total of 1.5 million cubic yards of sand were pumped ashore. Despite all of these efforts, the ocean had reclaimed nearly 125 feet of the shore and the Atlantic Ocean was within 75 feet of the tower by the fall of 1980.

Early erosion control efforts involved the installment of brush fence at the Cape Hatteras Lighthouse, as shown here in 1938.

The Cape Hatteras Light Station included dwellings for both principal and assistant keepers. The double keepers' quarters, built in 1854, housed two assistant keepers and their families. Today, the double keepers' quarters house the Museum of the Sea. The principal keepers' quarters, constructed in 1871 from material left over from the present-day lighthouse, accommodated the head lighthouse keeper and his family. The principal keepers' quarters now serve as a park office. The 1965 image above shows both dwellings, with the double quarters at left and the principal quarters at right. The 1955 image below features the principal quarters in the center of the photograph.

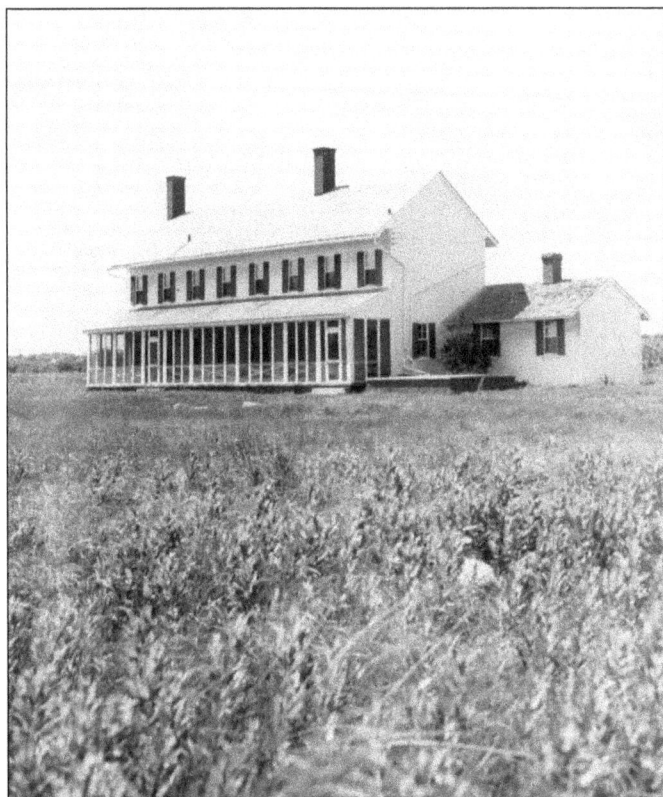

During Mission 66, the National Park Service established its main museum in the former double keepers' quarters (pictured at left in 1948) at the Cape Hatteras Light Station, which later included exhibits interpreting the history of the US Life-Saving Service and the Coast Guard. The image below, also from 1948, shows both the principal keepers' quarters (foreground) and the double keepers' quarters.

The Ocracoke Light Station, built in 1823, is pictured here in 1960. The lighthouse is 75 feet tall, and its diameter narrows from 25 feet at the base to 12 feet at its peak. The walls are solid brick and 12 feet thick at the bottom (tapering to two feet thick at the top). An octagonal lantern crowns the tower and houses a fourth-order Fresnel lens. The exterior of the lighthouse was cemented and whitewashed in 1868, giving it the appearance it has today. The original whitewash "recipe" called for blending lime, salt, Spanish whiting, rice, glue, and boiling water; the mixture was applied while it was still hot. This is the oldest operating light station in North Carolina.

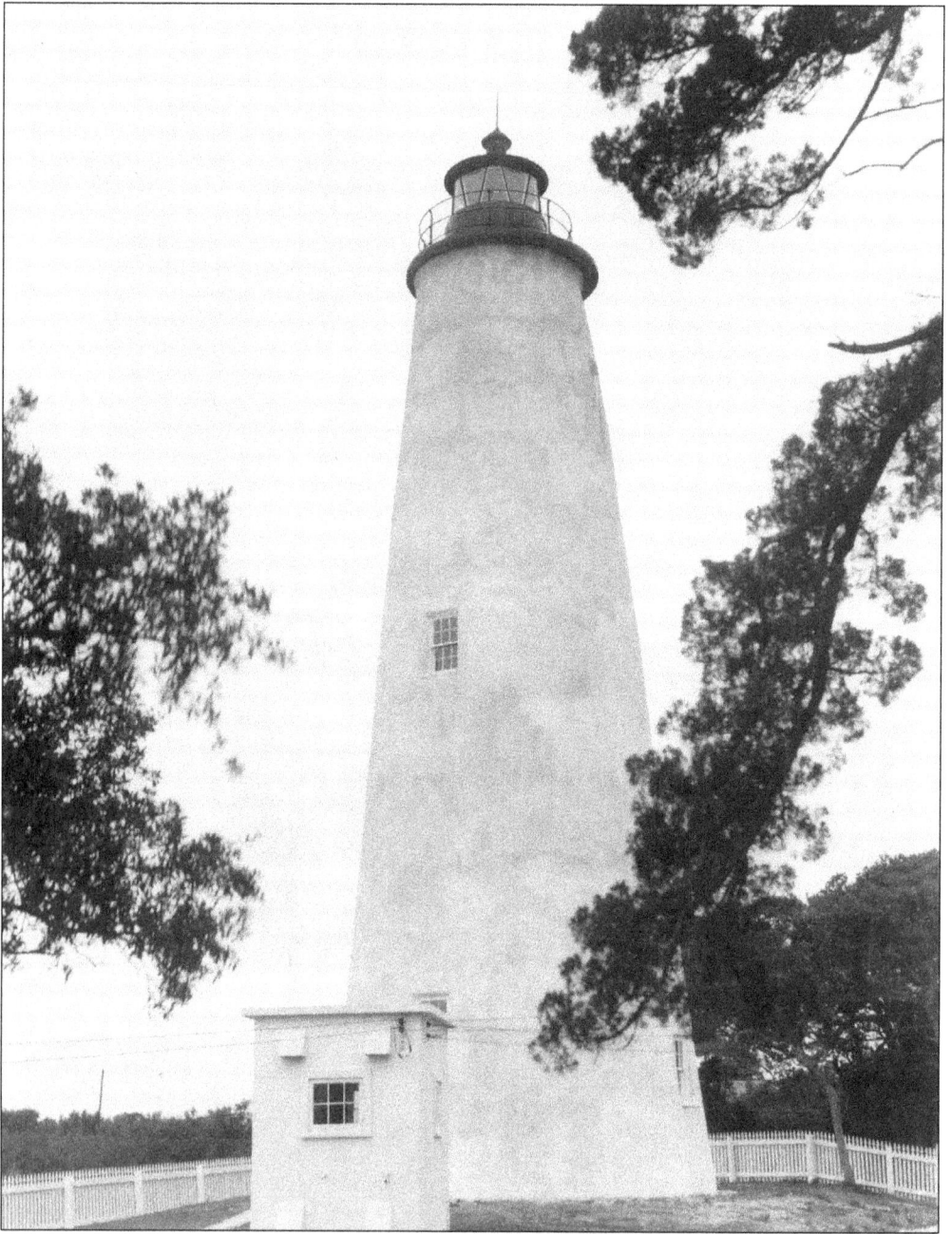

The Ocracoke Lighthouse was automated in 1955. The original staircase was a wooden-step spiral staircase built into the inside of the exterior wall. During the 1950s, the rotting wooden staircase was replaced with a less substantial metal spiral staircase. The Ocracoke Light Station was added to the National Register of Historic Places in 1977; this photograph was taken in 1952.

This 1952 image shows the two-acre Ocracoke Light Station Historic District. In 2000, the US Coast Guard transferred ownership of the Ocracoke Lighthouse to the National Park Service. Today, the Coast Guard maintains the 1854 fourth-order Fresnel lens as a functioning aid to navigation, while the National Park Service maintains the lighthouse as a historic structure.

As duties increased at the Ocracoke Light Station, the US Coast Guard established an assistant keeper position. To house the additional keeper and his family, a second story was built onto the original quarters in 1897, and another section was added in 1929. Today, the double keepers' quarters are used as housing for park staff. The shed on the left in this 1952 photograph is no longer standing.

Ocracoke Light Station keepers fished, raised livestock, and planted gardens near their quarters. Due to the proximity of the village, the keepers and their families enjoyed a social life in Ocracoke, and their children were schooled in the village. The above image shows the light station in 1950, while the image at left is from 1936.

The Bodie Island Life-Saving Station (1878) is located on the southern end of Bodie Island within Cape Hatteras National Seashore. The structures were listed in the National Register of Historic Places in 1977. In 2008, the 10 acres of the Bodie Island Life-Saving Station Historic District, including the 1916 boathouse and the Bodie Island US Coast Guard Station, were relocated from near the ocean north of Coquina Beach to three miles south of the entrance to Bodie Island Light Station on Lighthouse Bay Drive. This photograph was taken in 1988.

The Bodie Island Life-Saving Station and boathouse (pictured in 1980) were turned over to the National Park Service in 1953 at the time of the establishment of the national seashore. Today, the structures are used as office space for the Bodie Island Park Rangers and storage for the boathouse.

The Bodie Island Life-Saving Station and boathouse are pictured undergoing repairs and restoration in 1955.

The Bodie Island Life-Saving Station (pictured during its 1955 relocation) was used for the park superintendent prior to its move down the beach, due to ocean erosion threatening the structure.

The Bodie Island Life-Saving Station boathouse was built in 1916. The boathouse was relocated down the beach a few miles in 1955 and has undergone some modifications over the years.

The original name of the 1878 Bodie Island Life-Saving Station (pictured in 1955) was Tommy's Hummock Life-Saving Station. Several life-saving stations were called "Hummock"—a general geological term referring to a small knoll or mound above ground in a high dry area in a swamp.

The Bodie Island Life-Saving Station (pictured in 1955) was converted to a residence when the US Coast Guard station was built nearby in 1925.

Pictured in 1952, the towers of Loran Station, constructed between 1944 and 1949, once dotted the landscape near the Bodie Island Life-Saving Station. The Loran radio navigation system operated over long distances. Synchronized pulses were transmitted from widely spaced radio stations to aircraft or shipping vessels: arrival time of the pulses was used to determine position.

The Bodie Island Coast Guard Station was built in 1925. The 10-acre Bodie Island Coast Guard Station and Bodie Island Life-Saving Station Historic District includes the Bodie Island Life-Saving Station, the US Coast Guard station, and the station watchtower, which is no longer standing. This image is from 1962.

The Bodie Island Coast Guard Station watchtower was removed after it was damaged by a storm in 1962. The tower was originally located behind the station.

The Bodie Island Coast Guard Station (pictured in 1958) was used as the Cape Hatteras National Seashore headquarters after it was transferred to the National Park Service from the US Coast Guard in 1953. Now, after the building's move in 2008, the structure is once again used as office space for park staff.

The Bodie Island Coast Guard Station (pictured in 1958) was listed in the National Register of Historic Places in 1977. In 2008, the two-story Coast Guard station was relocated from its beachside site north of Coquina Beach to the west side of the highway. It now sits at the entrance of the Bodie Island Light Station on Lighthouse Bay Drive.

This 1948 aerial view shows the 1925 Bodie Island Coast Guard station, the 1878 life-saving station, and the Bodie Island Loran Station towers (in the background).

This 1935 image shows the Bodie Island Coast Guard Station.

The US Coast Guard station at Oregon Inlet (pictured in 1952) began as a life-saving station in 1883 and was originally located south of the inlet on Pea Island. By 1988, the old station was completely abandoned by the Coast Guard, and a new station was constructed north of the inlet near the Oregon Inlet Fishing Marina. The North Carolina Aquarium now owns the old station.

The Pea Island Life-Saving Station (pictured in 1960) was the first life-saving station in the country to have an all-black crew, and its captain, Richard Etheridge, was the first black man to command a life-saving station. Decommissioned in 1947, the station was located in the area of what is now the Pea Island National Wildlife Refuge. In 2006, the Pea Island Cookhouse was moved to Collins Park in Manteo, North Carolina; the Pea Island Preservation Society now manages it.

This 1956 aerial view shows the Chicamacomico (pronounced *chik-a-ma*-COM-*i-co*) Life-Saving Station, located in Rodanthe. This was an active US Coast Guard facility from 1915 until 1954. Today, the Chicamacomico Historical Association manages the station as a historic site.

This 1956 photograph shows the 1910 Chicamacomico Surfboat No. 1046, used in the 1918 SS *Mirlo* rescue, at the Chicamacomico Life-Saving Station.

Little Kinnakeet (pictured in 1970) was one of the first seven life-saving stations erected on the Outer Banks of North Carolina. The site remained active under the US Coast Guard until 1954, when it was decommissioned and transferred to the National Park Service as a part of Cape Hatteras National Seashore.

The 10 acres of the Little Kinnakeet Life-Saving Station Historic District (pictured in 1970) include the 1874 boathouse, the 1892 kitchen, and the 1904 station house. A partial restoration of the historic structures has been completed to reflect the period of significance from 1885 to 1915.

The restoration of the 1874 Little Kinnakeet Life-Saving Station boathouse included removal of the addition to the structure and restoring the structure its appearance during the period of significance from 1885 to 1915. This photograph was taken in 1970.

This 1965 aerial view of the Little Kinnakeet Life-Saving Station includes the 1874 boathouse, the 1892 kitchen, and the 1904 station house. (Photograph by the US Coast Guard.)

Little Kinnakeet served as a quarters building for a park ranger in 1958. In 1900, the Kinnakeet Life-Saving Station was moved to the west side of the highway (to what is now mid-island). The Southern-pattern main station building was added to the southeast corner of the grounds in 1904.

Big Kinnakeet Coast Guard Station (in operation from 1878 to 1929) was damaged in a 1944 hurricane and demolished in the 1960s. Today, only the foundation exists within Cape Hatteras National Seashore. This photograph shows the station at its location—south of Avon, near Askins Creek—in 1934. (Photograph by the US Coast Guard.)

The former Cape Hatteras US Coast Guard station at Buxton, North Carolina, consists of two buildings that serve as an administrative office and garage, respectively. The station (pictured in 1965) is located one mile south of the Cape Hatteras Lighthouse, near Cape Point. The office is currently used as a park ranger station. (Photograph by the US Coast Guard.)

The US Coast Guard acquired the land for the Cape Hatteras Station (pictured in 1960) on May 29, 1937. In 1985, the National Park Service (NPS) took over the station buildings from the Coast Guard. In June 2004, the property, including several former Coast Guard administrative and maintenance buildings, was transferred to the NPS. (Photograph by the US Coast Guard.)

The Cape Hatteras Loran Station was constructed in 1949. The Cape Hatteras Lighthouse is visible in the distance in this 1950 photograph.

The Cape Hatteras US Coast Guard station and lookout tower are pictured here in 1939.

On May 14, 1942, during World War II, the HMS *Bedfordshire* was torpedoed and sunk off Ocracoke Island with all hands lost. Four bodies were subsequently found and buried on Ocracoke at the Ocracoke British Cemetery. Two of the gravesites are marked "unknown," and the other two bear the remains of Thomas Cunningham and Stanley R. Craig. The second British cemetery, known as Buxton British Cemetery, is located in Buxton on Hatteras Island near the Cape Hatteras Lighthouse, where two sailors from the British merchant vessel *San Delfino* are buried. Only one seaman was ever identified. Both of the graves are marked, but one is for the unknown seaman.

Cape Hatteras National Seashore contains seven old cemeteries, including this one (pictured in 1945). Most of the cemeteries have headstones that are over 100 years old, and some have just one cross marker.

Five one-story, wood-frame houses were designed by the National Park Service and built by the Civilian Conservation Corps (CCC) between 1939 and 1940. The cabins, pictured in 1942, are located within the Cape Hatteras National Seashore near the Cape Hatteras Lighthouse.

The CCC cabins were intended as overnight summer rentals for visitors to Cape Hatteras. Today, the cabins are used as housing for park staff. The CCC cabins are listed in the National Register of Historic Places. The wood-frame buildings, pictured in 1942, are distinctly plain with simple decorative cornices and large brick exterior chimneys.

The Hatteras Weather Bureau Station (pictured in 1960) in the village of Hatteras, North Carolina, was built in 1901 for what was then called the US Weather Bureau. The station played a key role in the nation's developing meteorological network until it was decommissioned in 1946. Today, the Outer Banks Visitors Bureau operates it in partnership with the National Park Service as a historic site as well as an information center. The Hatteras Weather Bureau Station is listed in the National Register of Historic Places.

The Hatteras Weather Bureau Station provided data on conditions in the Atlantic Ocean. The building served as a weather station and quarters for US Weather Bureau personnel from 1902 to 1946. In 1952, the property was turned over to the US Coast Guard, which used it until 1958, when it was transferred to Cape Hatteras National Seashore. The structure, pictured here in 1950, was restored in 2005 to its original 1901 design.

The Hatteras Inlet US Coast Guard Lifeboat Station (pictured in 1949) on Ocracoke Island was destroyed in a 1955 storm. The station was located near the current Ocracoke ferry dock; pilings are all that remain of the station.

The Mission 66 Ocracoke visitor center, grounds, and piers are pictured here after rehabilitation on May 22, 1957. During World War II, Ocracoke served as a location for a Navy section base from 1942 to 1944 and as an amphibious training station from 1944 to 1945, as well as a combat information center. In the 1960s, Congress transferred the old Navy docks on Ocracoke Island to the National Park Service for inclusion in Cape Hatteras National Seashore.

This photograph shows the Ocracoke Visitor Center in 1955. Just outside the village of Ocracoke, within Cape Hatteras National Seashore, is Loop Shack Hill, where the Navy monitored an underwater antisubmarine magnetic cable and maintained sensitive communications with other military installations.

The Ocracoke Coast Guard Station, constructed in 1940 and pictured in 1955, was vacated in 1996. The three-story, 17,000-square-foot station had been vacant for about five years when the 1.55-acre property and buildings were transferred from the federal government to the State of North Carolina; the North Carolina Center for the Advancement of Teachers (NCCAT) now uses the space.

Five

A CHANGING SEASHORE

In this image, a Cape Hatteras National Seashore visitor looks at the ocean near a disappearing barrier dune. The foreseeable future of Cape Hatteras National Seashore will depend on protection of eroding shorelines, financial resources, sea level rise and climate change, long-term sustainability of historic structures and public access to the beach, and seasonal beach closures to protect threatened or endangered species.

Shipwrecks off Cape Hatteras National Seashore range from the Spanish ships of the 1500s to boats of the Civil War and both World Wars, including the German U-boats. This photograph shows the wreck of the *George A. Kohler* of Baltimore. Driven by storm wave and 90-mile-per-hour winds during a hurricane, it was wrecked and washed ashore in August 1933.

The Liberty ship *Antonin Dvroak* ran aground two miles north of Little Kinnakeet Station on March 28, 1959, along Cape Hatteras National Seashore. The ship was later salvaged for scrap.

Shipwrecks along the 70 miles of Cape Hatteras National Seashore have seen ships broken to fragments and scattered, with a few large pieces remaining. Most wrecked ships are buried from sight for months at a time by surf or drifting sand only to be uncovered later. The 1921 wreck of the *Laura A. Barnes* (pictured in 1960) is accessible from the Coquina Beach parking area and may be visible in the dune line.

Today, most of the seashore shipwreck remains are visible only after hurricanes or big storms. Shipwreck timbers are protected by law as archeological resources. The shipwrecks are slowly disappearing due to exposure to the elements.

In 1967, large nylon sand-filled bags were placed in front of the Cape Hatteras Lighthouse in an effort to halt erosion. In 1969, the US Navy built reinforced concrete groins to protect the Navy facility and the lighthouse. (Photograph by Aycock Brown.)

In June 1999, the National Park Service began the process of relocating the Cape Hatteras Lighthouse and its structures. A series of hydraulic jacks moved the lighthouse along a system of tracks in five-foot increments. In just over two weeks, the lighthouse (pictured in 1967) was moved 2,900 feet to its current location. The National Park Service has sponsored a number of efforts to save the lighthouse, including sand replenishment projects, construction of rock revetments, sandbagging, planting artificial seaweed, and even tearing up and dumping asphalt from the adjacent parking area. (Photograph by Aycock Brown.)

A 1973 storm undermined the Coquina Beach day-use facility on Bodie Island. Many hurricanes hit the Cape Hatteras National Seashore, including Donna, which struck on September 11, 1960. Donna hit the Outer Banks with winds over 100 miles per hour, causing extensive damage to dunes, buildings, roads, and vegetation throughout the park.

Cape Hatteras National Seashore is spending increasing amounts of funding on costly storm damage repairs to facilities. On September 6, 2003, Hurricane Isabel made landfall on the Outer Banks of North Carolina with winds of 105 miles per hour. The storm surge produced a 2,000-foot-wide inlet on Hatteras Island, isolating Hatteras from the road for two months. This photograph was taken in 1973.

North Carolina Highway 12, a vital transportation link along the seashore, is often covered by high tides and storms that block access to villages on Hatteras Island. The State of North Carolina currently has plans to replace the Bonner Bridge; persistent problems along North Carolina Highway 12 south of the bridge through Pea Island National Wildlife Refuge to Rodanthe continue to create a planning challenge.

Climate change will affect the future of the North Carolina barrier islands. The shape of the Outer Banks has changed over the centuries due to stronger storms, rising sea levels, and bigger waves. Changes in the islands' vegetation have also altered the topography of Cape Hatteras National Seashore. The Cape Hatteras Lighthouse is visible near the top of this 1975 photograph.

Keeping portions of Cape Hatteras National Seashore above sea level in the coming centuries will be a challenge for park planners and will require political cooperation of the part of federal, state, and county leaders. Cape Hatteras Lighthouse is visible in the background of this 1975 photograph of Buxton, North Carolina.

125

A line of vehicles outlines Cape Point in this 1975 photograph. The use of off-road vehicles (ORVs) is a traditional way for locals and visitors to enjoy the seashore's beaches and the waters of the sound for fishing and recreation. After protests over the number of "beach buggies" and trash associated with their use in the 1960s, park officials studied the possibility of changes, limitations, or even the elimination of ORVs from park beaches. Several subsequent ORV studies led to an interim management plan for ORV use.

Off-road vehicles (ORVs) are shown lined up at Bodie Island in 1975. The final special regulation for the management of ORV use at Cape Hatteras National Seashore became effective on February 15, 2012.The new ORV management plan and regulation designates ORV routes in a manner that will balance visitor use and protect and preserve natural and cultural resources while permitting the use of ORVs on seashore beaches. Drivers are required to obtain an ORV special-use permit and display it while driving on the designated ORV routes.

This 1980 image offers an aerial view of Pea Island National Wildlife Refuge looking south toward Rodanthe, North Carolina. Pea Island National Wildlife Refuge, located within the Cape Hatteras National Seashore boundary, includes 5,880 acres.

In this 1980 aerial view of Sandy Bay, Cape Hatteras National Seashore looks south toward Hatteras, North Carolina. The Cape Hatteras National Seashore comprises 24,470 acres.

SANDY BAY

127

Visit us at
arcadiapublishing.com

www.ingramcontent.com/pod-product-compliance
Lightning Source LLC
Chambersburg PA
CBHW080606110426

42813CB00006B/1425